Is It Poetry or Is It Rap

By

Anthony Charles Crittendon

Is It Poetry or Is It Rap

Copyright © 2004 Anthony Charles Crittendon
ISBN 1-888754-30-3

All rights reserved. No part of this book may be reproduced or transmitted in any form or by any means, electronic or mechanical, including photocopying, recording, or by any information storage and retrieval system without permission in writing from the publisher or author.

Produced & Published
For
Anthony Charles Crittendon

By
**Cane River Media
25785 Catalina
Southfield, MI 48075**

To Order: Send $12.00 To:
A. C. Crittendon
19714 Fleetwood
Harper Woods, MI 48225
or Call 313- 884-8444

Cover Design by Herbert R. Metoyer
Printed in the United States of America

FROM THE AUTHOR

This book contains a small collection of poems or rap from past and present. Its focus is on life and job experiences; break up of a relationship, and family and friends (associates). It also touches on alcohol abuse, substance abuse, and never giving up.

Having faith in God and starting a new relationship with him has given me the courage to try to do something that I have never done before. It is He who has given me this gift and kept me alive so I may share it with **ALL OUR CHILDREN.**

Recovery and addiction are mentioned quite a few times and I know this is a life long process. Even if you don't use yourself, the majority of people I know have family members who do. Whether it be an uncle, aunt, brother mother, or father etc., maybe this collection can provide some insight on what goes on. Alcohol and/or drug abuse of any kind can affect entire families and your own neighborhood.

At times, I still feel humility for things I've done in the past, but I know it is still possible to turn my life around. I'm not perfect and never will be, and I don't claim to be a saint. Yet, I know if I keep the faith, I will be much better than I was yesterday. I know today, that when your mind is poisoned with mind altering substances including alcohol, it changes your perception and decision-making. At times, I would do things without taking the consequences into consideration.

I purposely included some poetry or rap from the 70s to show how I, as a young black man in America, felt during that era. I felt it was necessary to show who I was and wondering honestly if I have changed.

I've made many, many mistakes in the past, but It's time for me to move on and GROW spiritually and mentally at an accelerated rate.

A few people have asked me why I would open up some embarrassing situations which could cause me ridicule.

MY ANSWER: I want to help ALL OUR CHILDREN young and old, rich and poor; not to make the same mistakes I made and to let them know if they have a goal to keep trying — that it's never too late.

Acknowledgments

Special thanks to God for letting me open my eyes to see another day.

To my late grandparents, Robert & Willie Mae Flennory.

To my parents Roy and Nellie Mae Crittendon for obvious reasons. To my daughter Shannon (who's almost grown). To my sisters, Denise and Ernestyne and brothers, Roy Jr. and Baby Ray.

To Co-workers, Luther Chism, Debbie Randall, Billy Bridges, Veronica Knight, AL Horne, Lawrence Allen; Jackie Brown, Clayton Glover, Eddie Slaughter, Chris Gross, Rick Shepard and Rex Shrewsbury for words of encouragement during troubled times.

Very special thanks to counselors, Lynda Donald and Gregg Hughley; Also technicians Felix, Bruce, and THE LATE GREAT NATE.

Special thanks to New Hamburg, Joe, Ed, Steve, Carla, John W. Maxzine, Randy, Martin and the Late Darryl for support.

Special thanks to Claude Williams, Mark Carter, Jim Saros, Asha Tyson, Lee Drew, Red Ramsey, Pam Looney, Charlie Williams, Alvin Clavon, Arthur Lyles, Claire Horton, Denise Wunderlich Robert, and Teresa.

Also supervisors Paul Bohn, Kenneth W. Clavon, Young Dennis Frank Collins, and Josh Zimmer who **is** directly responsible for inspiring me to write "**Exactly 3 Seconds.**"

Even though we've never met, The Late Dr. King, Greg Mathis, Oprah Winfrey, Spike Lee, Marvin Gaye, Carlos Santana, and the Last Poets have inspired me greatly.

Last of all Lynette Hill-Johnson, Thomas Malinky, Kevin Mueller and Mike Kenney, THANK YOU.

TABLE OF CONTENTS

To Our Children	3
Once Upon A Time	4
Nellie May	6
Roy	7
My Death	9
Star	10
-uck You	11
Dedication For The Late Lonnie	12
Bled Man Walking	13
To Whom It May Concern	14
Shield Of Dreams	15
Dusty Black File	16
Shattered Dream Theme	17
Welcome Home	19
Remy	20
NO	21
Is It Poetry or Is It Rap	22
The Last Time	22
So Will I	23
Shannon	24
The Best Present	25
Baby Ray	27
This Picture	28
My Baby Mama	30
Esque	31
To Grandma	33
Rebirth	34
Another Chance	35
Ashley	36
Exactly Three Seconds	37
Tony The Tiger	38
Devin / Denise	40
Asha	41
Sport	42

Twenty-five and Under	43
Future NFL Pup	44
Double Dose	45
Nate	46
Maplegrove	47
Laugh Long	48
Just One Mile Apart	49
Vote	50
Almost Ready	51
Trying To Impress	52
Go Fishing — Cut Down A Tree	53
Cheap Clothes	54
The American Idle	55
Crittendon's Dictionary	56
25¢	57
Rumors Rumors	58
Favorite Song	59
Message To All Our Children	60
Artificial Flowers	61
Mouse Crap	62
Appreciation	63
White Collar	64
Judge and Jury	65
New Best Friend	66
Alive	67

TO OUR CHILDREN

This isn't a RELAPSE PREVENTION workbook
It's just a few words to tell what it took
I talk about a few people in life
Who knew me through my struggle and strife
I want to help OUR CHILDREN gain some knowledge
To be RESPECTFUL, EDUCATED and go off to college
That's not to say you need college in order to succeed
You can EDUCATE YOURSELF if you take timeout and READ
I hope they don't make the same mistakes I made
I hope they study HARD to get a better grade
And to let people know what I've done to myself
Instead of trying to put the blame on everybody else
Also to let OUR CHILDREN know that if they slip and fall
Turn to GOD and he'll let you STAND TALL

2/18/04

ONCE UPON A TIME

There was a little Black Boy
Who played sports just for joy
The school he attended had quite a few
So he even played soccer and hockey too
And only time would tell
Whether he did them very well
As time went on, he did them less
Because he realized he was 2nd best
Even though he worked his way through school
He often wondered what would make him cool
Pretty soon those college days came
And he hadn't received his much needed fame
With a tear, he traded in his football gear
And decided to sip on some beer
Those sips turned to gulps over a period of time
Then he decided to change to Wild Irish Rose Wine
After a while that didn't fulfill his need
So he decided to try some of this so called weed
More time….. College just didn't work out
Decision…. Let's see what the factory is all about
This work seemed to suit him well
Bought a couple of houses then decided to sell
Then came failed relationships one after another
Good times, Bad times, Death of a brother
A baby girl of his very own
Who overnight decided she was grown
Material things seemed to come and go
So he changed his ways and got 6 clean years in a row
Even though he had a better life
He thought he had a lovely wife
UH OH ….dishonesty is more than any man can take
Once again, he had made a mistake
He realized he had been thrown off course
So he decided let's get a divorce

The break up caused him a lot of pain
That's when he started acting insane
Drinking and partying among other things
Near fatal situations, that's what it brings
To get back together, it took about a year
The results will be determined in these pages RIGHT HERE

03/09/04

NELLIE MAE

*73 years ago on this day
A child was born named
Nellie Mae.*

*She raised four children by herself
Never asking for help from anyone else.*

*The oldest son who couldn't use a hammer
Became an established computer programmer.*

*Her only daughter became a writer with much success
Always trying to do her best.*

*Another son went to the auto industry
He's far from perfect, but he's trying to be the best he can be.*

*A few years ago God sent the youngest son home
To play with the angels, so he's not alone.*

*A church going lady who never feared the devil
Just for that they should give you a medal.*

*September 28th is a special day
Let's pray for a living angel called Nellie Mae.*

*And one more thing I forgot to say
"I love you, Mama…….Happy Birthday".*

09/28/03

ROY

Even though you only had one arm
You were known as the man with all the charm
Sometimes I have to sit and laugh
At things that happened in the past
Even though you didn't come to the game
I'm proud and honored we have the same name
I remember when I asked you for a pony
You said, "Where you gonna keep him at, Tony?"
I remember you sitting me in the high chair
And saying "Be still while I cut your hair."
I remember you picked me up when I fell
I also remember the ringing of the bell
I remember how I would get on your nerve
I remember when you taught me how to THROW THE CURVE
But many nights, I'd lay in bed and cry
Because you and Mama didn't see eye to eye
And now we both know divorce can be hell
Dad when you left, I wasn't even twelve
But the whipping's I got made me never forget
To treat the adults and elderly with respect
I'll never forget that whipping that day
When I flew your classic albums away'
The garage shingle Frisbee idea was all mine
When I finally climbed down you whipped my behind
And I'll never forget when you whipped my ass
When I asked for pay when you told me to cut the grass
Three times you told me to quit jumping on the bed
When you busted in with the belt I thought I'd be dead
I still remember every now and then
Praying for the Cleveland Indians to win
When they won, you were in a better mood, Dad
Then the whipping's wouldn't be so bad

Whipping's isn't what this is all about
I just wanted to let you know how I turned out
Dad, there's a few more things I've got to say
I'm glad I got those whipping's back in the day
Whipping's is what children need to know
It makes them respect and learn HOW TO THROW
Child abuse, child abuse, some people will shout!
But it worked better than TONY TIME OUT
That's what's wrong with the kids today
They think everything should be their way
Dad, I'm not bitter, not bitter at all
Whenever you want or need me just give me a call
Even though we live far apart
My love will always be in my HEART
I'm all grown up and I've slipped and fell
But I got up… How long… TIME WILL TELL
I never received my fortune and fame
But I'm MAN enough now to take the blame
A lot of people my age say they got their butt beat
But it taught them how to stand on their feet
All the whipping's I got were WELL DESERVED
And guess what Dad?… I can still THROW THE CURVE

02/26/04

MY DEATH

Did you know when I died?
Didn't you laugh at my funeral?
Did you rap with me that night
When my mind was confused and changing?
Did you know that I wanted to be accepted?
And that isolation was torture.
Did you know my strong points?
I'm sure you knew my weaknesses.
Did you understand my unique personality?
Or didn't you have the time.
Did you know that I loved you?
Did you really care?
Did you know that I'm physically alive and well?
It's just my mind that is mentally dead.

1/1/70

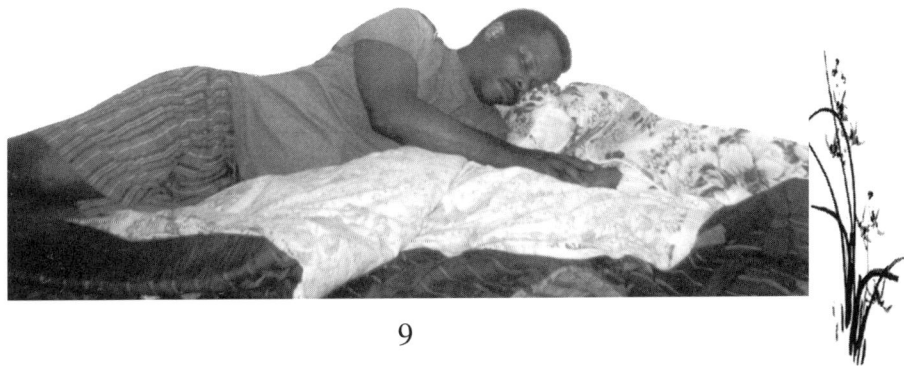

STAR

Seamless people on Times Square
Always bark that
It's bold
So cold
To reach for unreachable goals
But brothers
Sisters
Blend your mind
With mine
And start searching
For that perfect mold
Stay intact
With the fact
That you're a ...**STAR**
Without corruption
Or destruction
You will...function
And stay in touch
But remember
Remind **THE MAN UPSTAIRS**
That he gave you **TOO MUCH**

06/72

___UCK YOU

   __uck you, without a fight
because if you dream it seems you might.
I'm Black without an act
Coal Black and refuse to crack.
But mean green is more than a dream;
It willlllll help my scene…. it seems,
I'm gonna come ahead
My brothers blood has been shed and spread.
Listen…..
I can't spy or lie,
I'm not fried,
And I've tried, without a guide.
I can't hide,
And I'll never be denied; inside.
I'll always have my pride, on my side;
While you sit around and cry.
   __uck you,
you might as well have died.

                                                                     01/14/77

DEDICATION FOR THE LATE
LONNIE LAWSHEA, SR.

One of the greatest men I've known is gone from the world today
I'm sure that he had a lot more to do and say
He seemed to me, to be well known
And he fathered and raised ten children of his own
He constantly told them to do what's right
To grow physically and spiritually to see the light
Worked thirty long, hard factory years
And wasn't known to have any fears
He wasn't known to party, smoke or drink
The cause of his death makes me wonder and think
That the truth is hidden, there's a missing link
He was known for his love of kids all over town
Whoever pulled the trigger is pretty low down;
Shot in bed that's where he was found
Men like Uncle Lonnie are very few,
A man who could do anything he wanted to do
Uncle Lonnie, I'd be a great man too
If only I were more like you
This might sound bitter of me to say,

But I hope his killer goes the same way
This world is sick, maybe we all should pray
Because one of the greatest men I've known
Is gone from the world today.

01/25/77

BLED MAN WALKING

7 AM, while WALKING to visit the unemployment line
What I said to the police shouldn't be considered a crime
They screeched around the corner in their automobile
What was just about to happen didn't seem real
They searched my pockets and tore my black leather coat
Dissed me like my ancestors when they first got off the boat
They pushed me around like a broom and treated me pretty rough
That's when I got PISSED and said "I just about had ENOUGH!"
"WHAT'S THE PROBLEM AM I SPEEDING!!"
BOOM… BAM… BOOM, Now my lip is BLEEDING!
Now what in the HELL did I say that for
They started pushing me around rougher than before
Everything happened so quickly and fast
Then one cop said, 'OH…SO YOU'RE A LITTLE SMART ASS'
Then I felt a thud in my stomach and PAIN from a fist
I thought they'd kill and hide me so I'd never be missed
I didn't know this was part of their job
When he lied and said, 'YOU FIT THE DESCRIPTION OF A STORE JUST ROBBED!'
Yes, I had on a black leather coat and a gangster hat
But for what I said, I definitely didn't deserve all that
After they left… I continued WALKING to get my check
But this experience left me with a hateful bitter affect
God Bless America, in our RED, WHITE, AND BLUE NATION
Somebody please give me an explanation
I got my ass kicked by a couple of sick rednecks
I'M BLED MAN WALKING to pick-up my unemployment check
That was the first time that I've had that much ANGER AND RAGE
And the results were the words printed on the next page…

3/15/2004

TO WHOM IT MAY CONCERN:

For 200 years I've heard of red, white and blue. But for the sick rednecks I'm talking to, realize you're only fooling you. I've learned through my mind, and what you call crime, that red is dead; its something I said. You said white was alright, but you forgot that ten years ago I forgot about fright. I've turned to a mad, wild dog that's gonna bite, in spite of the fact that you call me midnight. I've got a feeling you can't control, it's called soul. I've reached a climax, but don't react to an ever-lasting fact. Oh yeah, I didn't tell you about blue, that's you because this time I'm really free. I don't grin at whatever you say, these 200 years are gonna be my way. I'm your bicentennial's nigga's grandson. Thank you fool, because I've listened and learned more from grandpa's school. "This time Its Midnight's Time To Rule." So be cool. I'll teach you how to pick cotton while you're tap dancing and shining shoes, then I'll give you a juicy piece of watermelon while you're sticking that needle in your arm. I'll treat you right when you graduate; the date is 2178. Right, you're my bait and don't be late.

P.S.
Do the best that you can do and write me back too, because I've learned a hell of a lot more than you.

Without A Doubt

01/16/77

SHIELD OF DREAMS

Even though it's been quite a few years
I had drank too many beers
I shouldn't have been driving my car
After drinking real heavy at the bar
2 AM while most people were in their jammies
I was determined to visit MY GIRL TAMMY
The other car had on high beams
When I first saw the SHIELD OF DREAMS
It only took a split decision
BAM!!…There goes a collision
Excruciating pain never experienced or felt
Because I decided not to wear my seat belt
With jagged glass lodged in my forehead
I struggled to open my eyes…I'm in a hospital bed
The results are one hell of a scar
Because I got behind the wheel of my car
I used to think I was kinda clever
But Mama said I lost marbles forever
Please children for heavens sake
Don't ever make this stupid mistake
Quite stupid of me it really seems
When I FELT THE SHIELD OF DREAMS

3/7/04

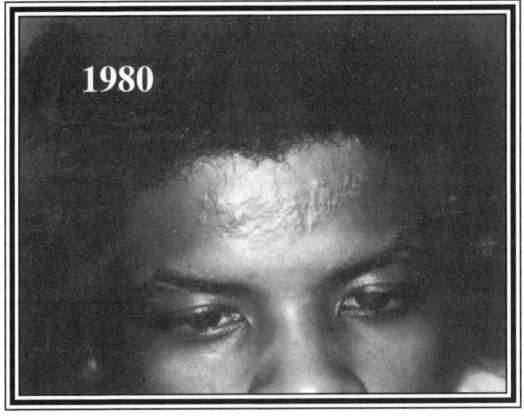

DUSTY BLACK FILE

Looking in my dusty black file
Searching for something to make me smile
Pulled out a folder that collected a lot of dust
A blue folder with the word that just said TRUST
In any relationship this is a must
Opened it up to see what I could find
It mentioned that you should be kind
and leave old skeletons far behind
I started thinking in my mind
That maybe it's just a matter of time
It also mentioned a word called Love
It said it should fit like a glove
That's when I looked to the sky Above
But all I saw was a wounded dove
Looking in my dusty black file
Made me believe it would be closed...
For awhile.

01/10/76

SHATTERED DREAM THEME

Six years sober and squeaky clean
How could you be so mean?
You shattered my dream, my ex-wife and dean
We grew apart, you broke my heart
With the deadliness of a poison dart
You shattered my dream you broke my heart
My wife forever, til death do us part
You shattered my dream
I should have known from the start
The graveyard shift is what I had to do
To make our lives better for me and you
Bought you a new car you thought was a cart
Shattered dreams you broke my heart
How in the hell did I get into this mess?
You say you want WHAT!! A Lincoln LS
House in the suburbs with the BIG backyard
What you did caught me off guard
WHY? Is that man in my house
You cried and pleaded for a second chance
Let's see if we can re-kindle the romance
26 one minute calls in 30 days
The only thing you could say is…'Hey Baby, I'm on my way'
Temptation set in. I had too much time to think
Now I guess I'll take a drink
Faced with another verbal attack
I listened to the devil and smoked some crack
I'm the plaintiff as everyone can see
But when the judge dropped the bomb it landed on me
Led down the road of resentment, self-pity, and shame
I know this relationship will never be the same
I prayed to God and dropped down on my knees
He told me Lifelong sobriety is the goal I must achieve
I was told 12 steps is what I should do
And respect relationships more than you

I've learned to listen and joined A.A.
With God's help I'll do what they say
A standing ovation isn't what I need
 To do what's right or a kindly deed
Now I can accept that it was all my fault, because I picked YOU
12 years ago, when I had more than a few
All is done and I wish you well
Even though some say you should go to HELL
Dedicated to my Dear ex-wife
Now leave me alone, let me get on with my life
Thanks for listening: and by the way
Now I can sing like Bill Withers, What a lovely day
You shattered my dream to the extreme
My ex-wife and a mouse named dean

06/21/03

WELCOME HOME

I thought this was home, But it's just a house
All our furniture is gone, even the couch

I thought this was home, But it's just a house
Because I don't really care for the mouse

I thought this was home, But it's just a house
Because I had a very disrespectful spouse

I thought this was home, But it's just a house
Does it hurt? Yes it does...............*OUCH!*

                                                           02/16/04

REMY

I like to run around and be free
I love to sit up under this tree
I just finished chasing a squirrel
Now where's that scary Alonda girl?
I can't stand this heat
I want something to eat
I don't have a lot of luck
My dad just left in his blue truck
He had a tear in his eye
Mama…is dad going to die?
I feel abandoned
Where's sister Shannon?
What's the real story?
I haven't seen Tyler or Tori?
What happened to Sadie?
That was my first lady
Where's Pam and Rick?
Is everybody sick?
Mama you said, everybody went away
Tell everybody I'm ready to play
I'm getting kind of lonely
I want my daddy, Tony
I really can't believe this
"UH OH"…I got to take a piss

Remy Crittendon
07/31/03

NO

Your picture won't appear in this book
No one will point fingers and say that's her, LOOK!

I don't mean to do you any harm
But it felt like you just cut off my arm

I'm doing much better since **'SHATTERED DREAM'**
When I had to blow off a little steam

I really don't mean to do you no harm
But I felt like I only had one arm

I guess it really isn't so bad
To be just like my dad

Even though it's only a figure of speech
There are some people I'm trying to reach

Even though I don't have a degree
I am happy, humble, joyous and free

God's given me a brand new way to live
And he's made it easy to forgive

Don't call me and tell me things I don't need to know
And Good Luck when you go to Bingo

No your picture won't appear in this book
No one will point fingers and say, that's her LOOK!

02/17/04

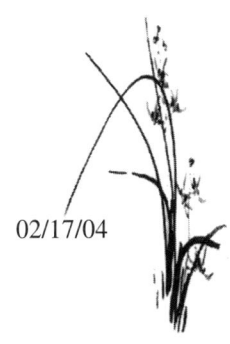

IS IT POETRY OR IS IT RAP?

Should I compliment her or say she's too fat?
Should I call her bitch or say she's all that?
Should I put her out or beg her to come back?
Should I try to solve the problem or try to attack?
    IS IT POETRY OR IS IT RAP?
Should I forgive her for stabbing me in the back?
Should I stay awake or should I take a nap?
Should I work long hours or try the illegal trap?
Should I hold my temper or should I just snap?
    IS IT POETRY OR IS IT RAP?
Should I try to change or should she adapt?
Should I stick it out or should I get my hat?
Should I be glad I finished writing this crap?
Should I scream yahoo! Or should I just clap?

                                              12/19/03

THE LAST TIME

The last time I take a sip
The last time you will see my lip
The last time I make my family cry
The last time I'll make up a lie
The last time I'll pretend to be sober
The last time I'll be hung over
The last time I'll be broke
The last time I'll take a toke
The last time I'll argue and rage
The last time I'll be put in a cage
The last time I'll play this game
The last time I'll find someone to blame
The last time I'll write about you
I've got to do what I've got to do
GOOD-BYE

                                                12/01/03

SO WILL I

Old ship sinks
So did I
Alcoholic drinks
So did I
Cons game
So did I
People blame
So did I
Babies cry
So did I
Addicts die
So did I
Losers use
So did I
People abuse
So did I
The water falls
So did I
Old car stalls
So did I
Jesus wept
So did I
Baby takes 1st step
So did I

God forgives
So will I
Servants give
So will I
A bird feeds
So will I
A reader reads
So will I
A new car will go
So will I
Grass will grow
So will I
The sun lights
So will I
A warrior fights
So will I
A teacher advices
So will I
The sun rises
So will I

So will I
So will I

03/24/04

SHANNON

A lot of class and a pretty smile
You will always be my child
Don't grow up to be illiterate and wild
Study hard is what I preach
Respect your elders, let the teachers teach
If you do, there's no goal you won't reach
Remember Shannon, I'm from the *"Old School"*
Where the parents made all the rules
Remember to thank God when you pray
Thank him for letting you see the next day
Always on the phone
And thinking that you're grown
Pretty soon you'll be out on your own
I know I'm strict and tell you what to do
But my love is tighter than the strongest glue
I'm not perfect, sometimes I show too much rage
I know you think I should be put in a cage
Later in life, you'll have kids of your own
Challenge what you say and think they're grown
One day that I can't wait to see
Is the day when you say "These kids were just like me."
Shannon, the good you do outweigh the bad
This is just something to think about
      It comes from your DAD

07/22/03

THE BEST PRESENT

Ever since you were a child and sat on my knee
I preached, be honest and never lie to me
Since you've grown older, we don't always agree
But remember material things don't mean that much to me
Respect yourself and others and you'll always be free
Now it's Christmas time and what do I see
Is a maturing young lady being the best she can be
Now that's the best present I can have

UNDER THE TREE

12/18/03

Baby Ray

BABY RAY

Very few words mentioned in the paper today
Black man pulled out the water of the San Francisco Bay
To you his killer, there's a few words I've got to say
You took a piece of my soul when you killed my Baby Brother Ray

He dressed different and had long hair, but that doesn't make him gay
Even though I don't know who you are, you think you got away
God PLEASE forgive me for what I'm about to say
But killer…you'd burn in HELL FOREVER if I had my way

To you his killer I think that you're a beast
If I got my hands on you, you'd need the police
He never got to really know his nephew and his niece
You're a cold-hearted coward to say the very least

If I had a pound of RAT POISON I'd serve you up a feast
And to wash it down I'd give you a mug of boiling hot grease
You're the reason that MY BABY BROTHER is deceased
I LOVE YOU BABY RAY   MAY YOU REST IN PEACE

There were 3 brothers now there's only two
If anybody knows his killer PLEASE give me a clue
The most I would really do is make him BLACK AND BLUE
I know the anger in the preceding lines never will come true

I'll pray for FORGIVENESS when I kneel down in the pew
Because God tells us to FORGIVE THEM 'FOR THEY KNOW NOT WHAT THEY DO'
A GIFTED AND GENTLE BROTHER I wish everybody knew
There's not a day that goes by that I don't say,

                BABY RAY, I LOVE YOU

03/08/04

THIS PICTURE

I Stared at this picture of you and him from the past
And it reminded me of the time you hobbled around with a cast

You were one of five passengers in my car that day
You, me, Chris, Jessica and, of course, Baby Ray

Even though the other driver was at fault when she broadsided my car
You were an artist, musician, and a drummer about to become a star

Permanent pins in your ankle and knowing you will never play the same
Not once did you imply or insinuate that I was the one to blame

You apologized to me when I was included in the lawsuit
I told you not to worry, you deserved to get your loot

Let the lawyers and the insurance company play their little game
Because it really didn't matter because our company was the same

You seemed more relieved than I, that she was guilty 100 percent
And you handled it all with class, like a scholar and a gent

Your career goals changed, but your dream to succeed never would fade
It showed with your fine work on floats in the Thanksgiving Day Parade

Many years have passed, but you recently visited my mother
And I recall you named your only son after my baby brother

At Baby Ray's farewell dinner, you took time enough to think
And was considerate enough to ask me, "Do you mind if I drink?"

At times, I feel empty inside, knowing that he's missing
And try to think of happier times… when I start reminiscing

Cremation was his wish when he was laid to rest
And as friends go, I believe you and he were the best

Staring at this picture brought back many memories, I must confess
I wish you, your wife and family Much, Much Success

Jimmy, it has been many years since we've seen one another
You've proved that color doesn't matter, because
                            you're definitely a BROTHER

                                      06/26/04

MY BABY MAMA

Even though we never wed, and you were never my wife
God blessed us with a child to be in our life
I really didn't want to write about MY BABY MAMA
But if I don't, it will probably be a whole lot of drama
But I got to give you up, just like my KOOL MILD'S
Because our BABY GIRL is no longer a child
Even though it's been many years that have gone by
You complain about the way I do things…BUT AT LEAST I TRY
We argue too much, and seem to be too much alike
It's been that way ever since I bought Shannon her first bike
I did the best I could by myself for years, just about four
But I know now that raising a child is one hell of a chore
I'm not going to tell everybody about your story
You can tell it yourself, and get your fame and glory
But I've got to tell you something ON THE DOWN LOW
Shannon is almost grown…At least she thinks so
Even though we shout at each other and don't seem to jell
I wish you the BEST IN LIFE, but only time will tell
This might sound weird and maybe a little strange
But you'll always be my friend, THAT WILL NEVER CHANGE
Sharan, I'm not trying to write you a letter
But KEEP UP THE GOOD WORK and things will get better

02/23/04

ESQUE

Although you aren't my Pappy
You have made Nellie Mae happy

You and Mama never wed
But you've given me good advice for my head

Always up early in the day
You've spent 24 years with Nellie Mae

Always trying to be first at the bank
To you I just want to say…THANKS

Did you think I would forget about you?
NO WAY…NO WAY…ESQUE

02/27/04

Sister Willie Mae Flennory

TO GRANDMA

I'm apologizing to you with this little poem
Because it was your TEMPLE and not just your home
I really should have done this many years ago
But I was too ashamed to let anybody else know
This secret has been eating me up inside for many, many years
It happened after I had consumed too many beers
Really believing and thinking that I was all alone
I decided to get high in your Blessed and Sacred home
To some people it might not sound like such a big deal
But I'm just trying to be honest and to KEEP IT REAL
At the time, it didn't matter once that first drink was poured
But later on, I realized, I was getting high in the presence of the Lord
And from Heaven, I know and realize you were watching me all the time
So, I'm begging you for your forgiveness with this little rhyme
You always held a special place in my heart that was so unique and dear
So, I wanted to let you know that I really am sincere
As a child I felt safe and protected in your warm hold
"Believe in God And Do Right," is what I was told
So finally, I'm trying to do what I know is RIGHT
That's why I'm willing to write this apology down tonight
I know this little book will eventually come to an end
So, I really need and want to make this amend
Should I hide this poem so nobody will know?
No!! I'm trying to spiritually and mentally grow
This was one of the most ignorant, thoughtless acts that I've ever done
I'm TRULY SORRY GRANDMA… from your grandson
I've finally got this demon off my chest
Now my mind can be free, at peace and rest

06/28/04

REBIRTH

RECOVERY RE-BIRTH RECOVERY

Reading and
Re-educating
Re-adjusting and
Realizing
Remembering
Results
Retracing and
Returning to
Rediscover
Religion and
Responsibility
Re-creating
Respectability and
Rewarding
Results

RECOVERY
RE-BIRTH
RECOVERY

02/03/04

ANOTHER CHANCE

When the devil had me working for sin
You gave me another chance time and time again
When I didn't have money to afford a meal
You blessed me with a job so I wouldn't have to steal

Many nights I would drink til I was ill
The truth *is* in Your word, not a drink or a pill
When a foiled, spoiled relationship drove me insane
You lifted me up and eased the pain

When I was hurt and lonely in the middle of the night
You let me know everything would be alright
When I lied to my family about where I've been
You gave me another chance once again

Yes Dear Lord, You answered my prayer
When I thought life was so unfair
I now know I wouldn't be living today
If I didn't get down on my knees and pray

Sometimes I didn't deserve to get out of trouble
That's why now my love will double
You've saved other souls just like me
That's why today I'm humble to Thee

Recognizing You today is how I feel
You lifted me up and let me heal
It took too many years for me to see the light
That's why now I'll worship You day and night

Thank You Father... Your son forever

1-23-04

ASHLEY

She seems to be kind of young
And I don't know where she's from

But that's really okay
She always has something positive to say

A soft petite voice
And she's made the right choice

She's alcohol and drug free
A blessing…that's just like me

She has mesmerizing eyes
And slender bronze thigh's

When God made her he broke the mold
Sometimes I wish I wasn't so old

She seems to be well educated
Should I ask her out…well maybe

As simple as adding two plus two
By now you know I am writing about you

As fine as an actress on TV
A unique young lady they call Ashley

12/10/03

"EXACTLY 3 SECONDS"

Is there a problem Clutch City tonight?
Because you're white collar, does it
always make you right?
In my old half century eyes
Your wear a mask and a disguise

When I've got something really important to say
You tell me to "GET OUT" or you turn and walk away
And don't you ever, ever forget
When I started working here, you weren't born yet

I don't think much of your team morale
When you lie to my face, then pretend I'm your pal
There's something else you haven't learned yet
Treat employees fair and you'll get your respect

"EXACTLY 3 SECONDS" to get on my job
When you called security, you thought I would sob
It's been almost 30 years that I've worked here
I'm not real scary, I have *NO FEAR*

Dr. King and Mr. Reuther would roll over in their grave
If they knew the way leadership is trying to behave
I'm union pride tough, not soft like a peach
And in America, we do have freedom of speech

You and I aren't always going to agree
But boot camp tactics don't work with me
Things aren't getting any better
Why can't we all just work together?

I'm getting older now, I don't move so fast
Hey boss! Can I have "EXACTLY 3 AND HALF?"

02/06/04

TONY THE TIGER

I'm a tiger locked in a cage
Filled with bitterness, anger and rage
This feeling has lasted close to a week
But an apology was really all that I seek

I know I can't control what you say
But I came here to work not to play
Listen boss, I'm not your average Joe
I don't want to be your side show

I know I shouldn't write this down
But who ended up looking like the clown
I know I should mellow with age
But I'm a tiger locked in a cage

Everything you say isn't the law
That's why you saw my teeth and my claw
I don't like being dissed by someone half my age
I'm a wild tiger locked in a cage

I know holding resentments isn't good
But don't stereotype me as "IN THE HOOD"
This tiger isn't on the cereal box
This tiger graduated from the school of HARD KNOCKS

There's one more thing I didn't tell you about
One day this tiger is going to break out
And let me give you another tip
I don't like the sound of a whip

This kinda reminds me of Siegfried & Roy
I'm a grown man not a little boy
I know I can't control what you do
But guess what…? Neither can you

I finally got this off my chest
Now I'll leave it alone and let it rest
As you grow older you'll realize you're not the boss
The real ringmaster DIED ON THE CROSS

02/10/04

DEVIN/DENISE

I haven't seen you in quite sometime
I'll try to explain it with this rhyme
I came to your job and you weren't there
I wanted to let you know that I still care
Long ago when we met you said your name was Devin
When you smiled at me I thought I was in Heaven
Your charm and beauty melted my heart
And your beautiful figure was like a fine piece of art

I lusted for you, with desire
You started a small flame that turned into a fire
We talked for hours about things that hurt in the past
But then I wanted you forever, I thought it would last
I wanted you to be MY HONEY
But often wondered was it just for the money
Until the very, very end
Devin, you will always be my friend

I hope you won't be offended
But my desire for Devin has now ended
And there's one fact I can't avoid
I can't come to the place where you're employed
I hope you don't think that I'm a bore
But Devin, I DON'T WANT TO DRINK NO MORE
But Baby one thing you must not forget
The flame hasn't quite burnt out yet

Now that it's out, and my mind is at peace
I want to get to know my SWEET DENISE
And one more thing I forgot to say
I still want you, HAPPY VALENTINES DAY

02/13/04

ASHA

I shouldn't have left when you were gonna offer me some advice
Mama said I was hardheaded, "That's the Story of My Life"
When I think back it still makes me smile
That a Lady with your status would say, "Please stay awhile."
*When you hugged and thanked Mama for cooking **real food***
It was quite humorous and got me in a good mood
But I thought you were gonna say something I didn't want to hear
That's one of the side effects from too much liquor and beer

Even though it's been out of my system for quite some time
What I did was stupid, it should have been a crime
I told everybody I had something else to do
But deep down inside, I thought everybody knew
That bottle on the table that the other guys were drinking
Had me doing some of that STINKING THINKING
And maybe I was embarrassed by things I've done in the past
Wondering what questions you might ask

Maybe I felt bad because I haven't had any success
And thought you'd quiz me, then give me and test
Maybe I'm a little crazy, maybe I'm a nut
And maybe I don't care about who has what
Maybe I felt uneasy and didn't want to grow
And maybe I knew you had been on Oprah's TV show
Maybe I was the only one who didn't have a degree
And maybe I didn't want to embarrass my family

A lot of TRUTH is what's in "ALL OF THE ABOVE"
But "THANKS" for trying to show a little bit of love
May be it's coincidental, I really can't say
*But in the meantime have a **HAPPY VALENTINES DAY***

2-14-2004

SPORT

If I pulled you from the lake with a hook
Would people stare, would people look?
If I did it to you I'd be in court
Is fishing considered a sport?

If I shot you down with a gun
When you were desperately trying to run
If I did it to you I'd be in court
Is hunting considered a sport?

If I shot you down with a gun
When you were desperately trying to run
If I did it to you I'd be in court
Is war considered a sport?

If I bombed your hometown
And your family was never found
If I did it to you I'd be in court
Is terrorism considered a sport?

01/12/04

25 AND UNDER

I'm an OLD DOG and you're just a PUP
If RAP wasn't mentioned in the title, would you have picked it up?
It doesn't seem that long ago that I was twenty-five
Partying my ass off and trying to survive

Now that those years have doubled from Blessings from the Lord
I got something to RAP about, a fact that can't be ignored
There's many rough roads in life… not all is peaches and cream
Education and prayer can help you fulfill your DREAM

The fact is very few will ever work at companies like Ford
There's a whole lot of other opportunities out there to be explored
And you say, you're grown now because you've reached a certain age
But it's hard to raise a family on the minimum wage

Oh yeah: POETRY AND RAP are the same basically
Finish reading the book then you'll see
So listen to your RAP and let the lyrics flow
But take some advice along the way
    from the OLD DOGS that should know

02/23/04

FUTURE NFL PUP

This old dog finally learned a new trick
A pup had to show me how to get up quick
We both passed through doors at the same place
But he refused to hide his face

He held his head high and refused to be defeated
While I held resentments, lied, and cheated
But I don't have to worry about the media and the press
And tell them how I got into this mess

I don't have 70,000 people who know about my past
I'm not the first and I won't be the last
While I watched his progress from a distance
His performance was flawless and persistent

Like Alecia says, "YOU DON'T KNOW MY NAME"
He's out there playing one Hell of a game
Now I'm really starting to understand
That I'm no more important than a grain of sand

So pup even though we never met
I see you as a *Triple Threat*
Courage, Heart, and Desire to succeed
It's something that all of us really need

So "GOOD LUCK" when you go to the NFL
Keep what you got and GIVE 'EM HELL
And THANKS for letting OLD DOG into the 2nd half of the game
And I'd say it's a safe bet, that you'll end up in the HALL OF FAME

02/24/04

DOUBLE DOSE

How much pain do I have to endure
Because I know this disease has NO CURE
If I don't really GIVE A DAMN
I'll go back to working MY PROGRAM

I've known this fact in the past
But went back out and let it whip my ass
That's what got me in the position I was in
Drinking, partying….committing a lot of sin

The way I see it. It's my decision
To keep my disease in remission
And if I want my chances to get better
I'll follow the A.A. program to the letter

This disease is fatal that's why I don't play
I call my sponsor every single day
The 12 steps also play a big part
Of keeping a beat in this heart

And if I don't attend meetings at least 5 times a week
My disease will spread and be at its peak
But to relieve all my symptoms of stress and strife
I remembered to put GOD back in my life

I know the Lord doesn't promise me that I'll wake up everyday
But I work too hard to let this disease make me pass away
I'm feeling real good now, and I don't mean to boast
Bill W. and Dr. Bob…I'll take a double dose

02/12/04

NATE

Sorry I didn't write sooner and it's taken so long
I was busy trying to accept the fact that I was wrong
And Nate here's a few words I never got to say
I've finally stopped trying to do it MY WAY
It seems like recovery is a much better life
Because I started accepting yours and others advice
I'll never forget the disappointment in your face
When I relapsed and had to come back to this place
Nate I wish your family only knew
All the problems I created, that you helped me through
You'd always say, "SOME OF US MUST DIE SO OTHERS CAN LIVE."
Nate...you had a whole lot to give
Even though those are words from someone in the past
When you said it...it stuck... I think it's gonna last
I'll never ever forget how I felt that day
When Lynda D. told me that you had passed away
When she told me it brought a tear to my eye
Because you and Felix were the ones that I could most 'IDENTIFY'
Things aren't perfect but they're getting much better
It started with your advice and the 'GOOD-BYE LETTER'
And one thing Nate I know for sure
Your words of encouragement helped me with a disease with NO CURE
Another reason I'll always be GRATEFUL to you Nate
You told me to be a MAN and step up to the plate
I still remember in the gym when you pulled me aside
And you told me I could run but I could not hide
I'm sorry Nate that I didn't get a chance to say "GOOD-BYE"
I've got to stop writing now because I don't want to cry
And if you're wondering how I'm doing, I'm doing just great

Thanks to God....A.A. and MY BROTHER NATE

02/11/04

MAPLEGROVE

Just like a half dozen eggs frying on the stove
That's how my mind was when I returned to MAPLEGROVE
You already taught me the consequences of alcohol abusing
But I went back out and kept on using

I was hardheaded and came back a couple more times
My pockets were pretty empty, I think I had two dimes
I used to think I was a tough guy from the Motor City
But I was here practicing resentment and self-pity

Many times I felt that you had too many rules
I had to go to the gazebo just to smoke my KOOLS
But now I know I was blessed to have had that seat
The half dozen eggs frying needed some meat

Many don't cook because they have a lot of fear
Many don't cook because they're gulping liquor and beer
Then I started thinking…a half a dozen eggs starting to fry
Hmm…only one dozen steps for me to apply

Put some MEAT with your eggs and never try to fake it
Tell'em to turn up the heat, in fact let'em bake it
I was taught as a small child never to waste
So last time, I cooked and seasoned my MEAT to taste

MAPLEGROVE you're the MEAT that made my belly full
You saw through all my lying, whining and bull
As treatment centers go, you're number one
You're the MEAT I needed…and I like mine WELL DONE

03/05/04

LAUGH LONG

Just as long as the neck of a giraffe
Some of my co-workers are starting to laugh
So now you're a rapper and started to chuckle
I felt like giving him a mouthful
of knuckles
One worker said, "I ain't never
seen a poet get rich."
And I thought to myself, *AINT
THIS A BITCH*!
When I told him that's not why
I'm writing this book
He gave me that, *THAT
NIGGA'S CRAZY* look
And when he had that laugh and
smirk on his face
I was shocked and astounded,
we're the same race
But there are a couple of people
who don't doubt
They really BELIEVE that everything will all work out
Co-worker Bill said, "Tony, you missed your calling."
He had no idea in the past, I was slipping and falling
And then awhile later, I got a little more relief
When Big Luther said he had some belief
This project I've taken on has made me feel brand new
Even if I only inspire very, very few
Message to ALL OUR CHILDREN when your peers put you down
Remember, soon you will walk tall and proud in your cap and gown
Just like a giraffes neck is long
I'm going to prove to them that they are WRONG!

02/18/04

JUST ONE MILE APART

GOD knows I've been trying to be humble
But I've got to get this out, and I'm not going to mumble
Dr. King, I know it would break your heart
If I told you about the meetings just one mile apart
The point that I'm trying to attack
The 1st meeting was 99% BLACK
DR. KING was it really worth the fight
The 2nd meeting was 99% WHITE
I'm aware that we shouldn't care
What color a person is when they share
We all have the same disease
Where is all the DIVERSITY?
This disease doesn't discriminate rich or poor
Keep on using, we won't have a key to any door
What's the problem, who's to blame?
All the stories are just about the same
If we don't recover, we won't be able
To share anything at any table
Don't you think it's a little odd
While practicing the steps we mention GOD?
I thought this was a melting pot?
But the truth remains...IT'S NOT
I like to go to different places
Where I can see different faces
The message that I'm trying to reach
Is we all should start practicing what we preach
Either place, I can 'IDENTIFY'
Either place, I've watched people share and cry
We all have an INCURABLE DISEASE
Let's start sharing together... PLEASE
Bill W, was this how it was supposed to be
One meeting for you and another for me
Dr. King I know it would break your heart
If I told you about the meetings just one mile apart

DIVERSITY   02/20/04

VOTE

You don't even have to spend a dime
And it only takes up a little of your time

I don't want to hear you say
Things really shouldn't be that way

One message I can't sugar-coat
Make some time to get out and vote

I'm talking to the young and old as well
While our taxes are going up high as hell

Don't complain about the politician
If you don't help make the decision

I don't want to hear all that chatter
Does my one vote really matter

Excuses I hear, the main complaint
I can't vote for him or her they're not a saint

While they're riding the rivers on yachts and boats
Get your ass up and make sure you vote

A nickel, a dime, what does it matter?
If we don't vote, their pockets will get fatter

02/23/04

ALMOST READY

Baby…why is that novel sitting up there on the coffee table?
Do you think I'm gonna read all that…do you think I'm able?

Baby I need something to read that's nice and short
If I wanted to just sit and wait, I'd go to traffic court

Just as long as the river they call THE NILE
It looks like I'm gonna be sitting here awhile

Baby! An hour has passed, you said, "You're almost ready."
"Come on let's go!! We're not going steady."

"Hurry Up Damn It! We're going to miss the next session."
You're as slow as the line of a funeral procession

You're the one who wanted to go to Bingo and try your luck
I'd have a JACKPOT if for every minute I waited, I had a buck

Well, you've taken so long, now I'm ready for a nap
Hey Baby! What's this other little book here called…
IS IT POETRY OR IS IT RAP?

Baby…why is that novel sitting up there on the coffee table?
The Hell with it, let's just sit here and watch some cable

02/25/04

TRYING TO IMPRESS

It puzzles me, I must confess,
But what did you lose up under that desk?
Who the hell are you trying to impress?
Boss-man I presume, it's just a guess.

Just like there are fish in the ocean,
Every time you work there's chaos and commotion.
You tell everybody that your job is your devotion.
But telling on co-workers won't get you a promotion.

You smell like a dead horse in a stable,
Always so ready willing and able.
Hey! Get up from under that table.
It's time to tell the boss a joke or fable.

You try to embarrass co-workers just to get a laugh.
Then you step on them until you wear a path.
There's not many people left to embarrass…do the math.
Something smells funny, I think you need a bath.

You talk real loud like the stereo Bose.
Running off at the mouth like a garden hose.
Maybe I shouldn't be so critical I suppose.
But Hey!…that smell…it's from that spot on your nose.

03/02/04

GO FISHING — CUT DOWN A TREE

I love to see the expression on their face
When the men come in and win at this place
She said, "Why don't you go paint the porch!"
I thought she was kidding, of course
My ex- is responsible for dragging me in this place
If you got something to say get in her case
They say that this is a woman's game
But me, I have no shame
Old lady said, "Go fishing, cut down a tree."
But I'm sitting here smiling with glee
It's more men than you might think
Dabbing away with their bottle of ink
I still love my PRO FOOTBALL
But occasionally, you'll see me in the hall
I became a great big fan
When they put that $GRAND$ in my hand
It's much cheaper than the casino
I – 26….BINGO!

"GO FISHING, CUT DOWN A TREE?"
Excuse me Baby…Let me count MY MONEY$$$

03/03/04

CHEAP CLOTHES

New school thinks I don't have no class
But I don't like artificial grass
I cut grass that grows and is green
But I don't wear no TOMMY JEANS
In fact, I don't even own a single pair
If they think I'm square, I don't care
And even if they don't agree
CHEAP clothes wear just fine with me
In style, what does it really mean?
It doesn't matter, as long as they're clean
You ask what those letters stand for?
And aren't those clothes just for the poor?
You're in your parents' house and car
What and who do you think you are?
Instead of always thinking about 'RAPPIN''
Let's get together and MAKE THIS HAPPEN
To buy these clothes, where do you go?
To tell you the truth, I really don't know?
But if you're interested, here's the LOGO

03/03/04

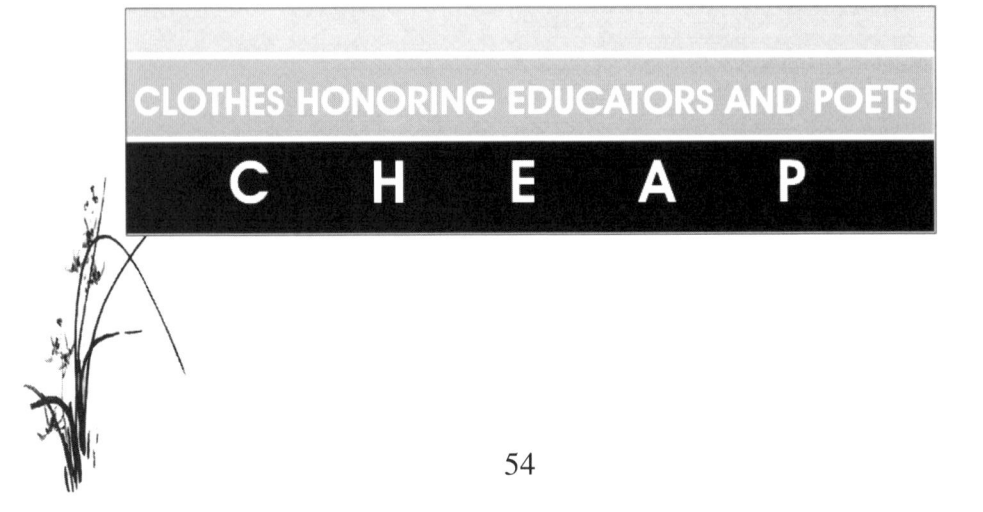

CLOTHES HONORING EDUCATORS AND POETS
C H E A P

THE AMERICAN IDLE

I knew when I first watched you training in camp
That you had the potential to be a hell of a CHAMP
You became the best CHAMP we've ever had
But it's really pitiful, in fact it's sad
Yes, you are THE AMERICAN IDLE
Refusing to relinquish your well deserved title
Now you're well known all over Motown
Because you proudly wear the belt and the crown
I held that title for a little while
And wore the belt and crown with a smile
But that smile turned into a frown
When the double cross you threw knocked me down
I really don't remember my last bout
That's something that they call a BLACKOUT
But I'm not going to bitch or pout
I'm glad that lifestyle knocked me out
Just like a Ford truck idling in park
Your mind is knocked out in the dark
When you finally decide to put down that drink
It will free your mind to be able to THINK
THE AMERICAN IDLE never being driven
Not using the gifts that you've been given
Ok CHAMP get off the canvas, off your lazy behind
God's blessed you with a gift it's called A MIND

03/04/04

FROM: CRITTENDON'S DICTIONARY
TO: ALL OUR CHILDREN

A NOTHER REASON
L OSER'S MEDICINE
C AREER'S RUINED
O NE AFTER ANOTHER
H INDERS PERCEPTION
O NLY TIME WILL TELL
L IQUID DEATH

A DDING PROBLEMS
N EVER GETTING ENOUGH
D ESTROYING FAMILIES

D ECIEVING
R EALITY
U NDERTAKERS
G RATEFUL
S ERVANTS

(ALC0HOL AND DRUGS)

03/12/04

C REATING
O NLY
N EAR FATAL
S ITUATIONS
E NDLESS
Q UESTIONS OF
U NFORGETABLE
E NDINGS
N O
C ONTROL AND
E VERLASTING
S ORROW

05/ 04/04

25¢

25¢ isn't a Brother Rapper
He's a man who used to be quite dapper
But that's before he stayed drunk and bent
PARTY, PARTY, but wouldn't pay rent
He used to say 'KEEP IT REAL'
And always drove a fine automobile
But one day he got too high
And decided 'LET'S JUICE IT UP AND FLY'

He didn't used to be that type
But he messed around and hit that pipe
He borrowed money from his family and only friend
Until they had no more to lend
Instead of trying to keep a job
An old man he tried to rob
That was a tough old buzzard he fought
And eventually he got caught

Like the wind blows a boat with a sail
He ended up spending time in jail
And the very day he was released
He begged a quarter from his niece
He really needed much, much more
So he decided to beg at the store
25¢ is a fictional name
And I'm used to your stupid con game

I want you to start to understand
That you've got to stand up and be a man
Everybody's met your type before
Standing around begging at the corner store
And don't ever ask me for a dime or quarter
In fact don't ask my teen age daughter
Get up, 25¢, and don't be defeating
And we'll RAP about it at the meeting.

3/12/2004

RUMORS RUMORS

Rumors, Rumors, boy do you need help
Rumors, Rumors, keep 'em to yourself
Last week you said, such & such's a fag
Every time you open your mouth, I want to stuff it with a rag

And you really need to keep that rag in your mouth
Because half the time you don't know what you're talking about
You're always trying to find someone weak to offend
Sometimes, you remind me of a cackling hen

Most of the time, you don't know what you're talking about
It won't be long before somebody knocks you out
You talk about people, both far and near
But don't tell me because I don't want to hear

When you find out the rumor that you spread was wrong
You're right back spreading another one twice as long
Rumors, Rumors, boy do you need help
If you want to spread rumors, spread'em about <u>YOURSELF</u>

2/20/2004

FAVORITE SONG

Carlos, you've played my all time favorite song
I listen to it whether things are going right or wrong

Through happiness, sadness, laughter and tears
I've listened to it for many, many years

I'll never forget when outside, I saw you '<u>LIVE</u>'
And the shrieks of your guitar made lighting in the sky

Carlos, I know you have many a hit
But when I first heard this…I knew this was it

Years ago, I told Roy Jr. to make sure it's played
At the final spot where my body will be laid

The sweet sound of your guitar soothes my soul
And it's helped me to fulfill a dream and a goal

When you play it, I wish it would never end
And the name of it is ***Song Of The Wind***

3/10/2004

MESSAGE TO: ALL OUR CHILDREN

Take your time, enjoy these years
Don't rely too heavily on your peers
Study hard, do your very best
It's gonna be hard, that's why they call it a test
Never give up, never give in
Don't wait for someone else to begin
Don't follow…take the lead
Don't expect praise for a kindly deed
Be proud and confident standing tall
Don't get your education at the mall
Listen to teachers, be ready to learn
So a decent wage, you will earn
Sometimes, you can bend, but never break
Do you realize your future's at stake?
Don't sass the teachers, they don't need you
They already have their degree…DO YOU?
Study HARD, you ask me why?
Or you'll work forever at Kentucky Fry
If you don't believe, if you don't agree
Your part-time job will be permanent at Mickey Dee

03/22/04

ARTIFICIAL FLOWERS

Like putting water on ARTIFICIAL FLOWERS in a vase
A mind is a terrible thing to waste

Don't give me a STANDING OVATION
For putting myself in this situation

Recovery isn't rocket science
I was known as "THE KING OF DEFIANCE"

I know sometimes I was a pain and a thorn
But recovery has made me feel REBORN

I know some will spit venom out of their mouth
But I'm not alone, look East, West, North, and South

And I'm not saying this in jest
But having a clear mind, I'll be at my best

Look North, South, East, and West
I know and pray this isn't my final test

The only way I can discover who I AM
Is to have FAITH IN GOD before my FINAL EXAM

Like putting water on ARTIFICIAL FLOWERS in a vase
A mind is a terrible thing to waste

03/15/04

MOUSE CRAP

This Isn't poetry this is <u>RAP</u>
I've got a present for you, It's called <u>MOUSE CRAP.</u>
Features of a man, but the character of a mouse
Don't worry about me and clean your own house.
Watching and harassing employees just for kicks
I heard the problem started around 1956.

This isn't THE CIVIL WAR, and you aren't General Lee
Why do you think and feel that you are better than me?
You consider yourself a Christian and a MANAGEMENT LEADER
You don't qualify to work at <u>K-MART</u> as a DOOR GREETER.
I hope there's not more like you…then we'd have MICE
Quit acting like the DEVIL, then pretending you're <u>CHRIST.</u>

This isn't poetry this is <u>MOUSE CRAP</u>
You lock yourself behind doors then take your <u>NAP.</u>
<u>THE TRUTH</u> will come out eventually, after the facts are reviewed
But at least I've got enough sense to get my license renewed.
You walk around smiling, pretending to be pleasant
And <u>THANK YOU</u> for time off as my 30 yr. present.

There's a couple of more things I forgot to mention
I know the company doesn't want to pay my pension.
It's been about 30 yrs. Since the day I was hired
And you're doing what you can to try to get me fired.
This isn't poetry this is my MY RAP
You're never going to succeed in trying to make me <u>SNAP.</u>

07-01-04

APPRECIATION

Thanks for showing me your appreciation
By unjustly giving me an unpaid vacation
It's the principle of the thing, don't you see
But it sure is strange how you just see me

I just saved the company a whole lot of money
But you gave me time off — you thought it was funny
What you did was a crying shame
I'm not a robot, I do have a name

You thought it would all blow over and I wouldn't make a peep
But "Hell, No!" I was not asleep
Yes, I did close my eyes
But the story you told was a bunch of lies

You think I'm stupid, but you're way off track
HA...., admit I'm guilty and we'll let you come back
"We're all in this together," that saying is so fake
Why are only white collars entitled to make a mistake

Thanks for letting me know how you feel
But no thanks, I don't want to cut a deal
You did what you thought you had to do
Maybe one day, I'll be **perfect**... just like you

06/01/04

WHITE COLLAR

I'm a father, union collar and a hard working man
Always doing the best that I can

Sometimes, I say things to try to help you out
But you're hard-headed and won't listen until I begin to shout

Remember, I've got 30 years out here on this floor
All slogans preach quality, but reality says *more*

I'm not going to sing a song like I'm in a choir
But you know I've got enough time to retire

Lack of communication, disrespect and a bad dream
Now you say you want me to be part of the team

I know my job "White Collar", listen, I'm not a rook
All my job experience didn't come from a book

Sometimes, I see a ring around your white collar
Because you want to cut my job just to save a dollar

If I question what you do, you think I'm trying to intervene
Why don't you take off that white shirt and go get it cleaned

Trying to put you down isn't my whole, sole mission
I'm just trying to get you to sit down and listen

Unbutton that white collar and treat me as an equal
Then there will be no need for me to write you a sequel

06/02/04

JUDGE AND JURY

The Judge and Jury live in the same house
I respect them as much as I do a mouse

Even though they haven't talked to you or me
They agree, and know what our sentence will be

They don't have time to listen to our innocent song
Because they already have proved that we are wrong

They treat you like a child or a cheap trick
I'm about to choke and gag because they make me sick

Sometimes, we sing softly and, sometimes, we sing loud
But, you'll never break our spirit — we're UNION PROUD

I often wonder what is your favorite color of paint
Because I already know what color it ain't

There's something I forgot to tell you... and there's no doubt
Eventually in time, the ***Real Truth*** will come out

The Judge and Jury live in the same house
I respect them as much as I do a mouse

06/03/04

NEW BEST FRIEND

My OLD FRIEND decided to get lost
Because he no longer could be the boss
He was a friend that I highly admired
But he actually was trying to get me fired

But just like a horse eats his hay
You said you'd be here to stay
Just like lemon goes with lime
You said you've been close all the time

You said you didn't feel appreciated
So you sat there and quietly waited
I'm glad I found you where have you been
I'm talking about my <u>NEW BEST FRIEND</u>

My OLD FRIEND I thought was on the level
Ended up working for the devil
He came in the form of a liquid
And soon became highly addictive

NEW BEST FRIEND, you're better than liquid in a cup
Even though sometimes I forget to pick you up
You've made me happier and things aren't the same
But I forgot to tell everybody your name

Let me introduce you to my NEW BEST FRIEND
He goes by first name only and that is…PEN

03/15/04

ALIVE

Chill bumps are racing all over and through my body.
    I don't know whether to laugh or cry
Now when you walk by me,
    I can look you straight in the eye
My body's no longer filled with substances
    that can cause me to die
I'm starting to feel emotion again,
    but a man isn't suppose to cry
I know I have sinned in the past,
    but guess what?... so have you
God's blessed me today,
    and he's the ONLY ONE I have to answer to
When people whisper behind my back,
    no longer will I crumble
Because I know I'm following the right path
    and learning to be humble
If you throw stones at my house,
    they'll probably sail right through
Because I left the doors and windows WIDE open,
    I did it just for you
There are long bumpy roads in life,
    as we travel from town to town
But remember God doesn't want us
    to KICK a man when he's down
It really doesn't matter
    whether you're YELLOW, WHITE, RED, or BLACK
Please open your heart
    and let's start giving it ALL BACK
We've got to start LOVING AND RESPECTING each other,
    that's my point of view
Because LOVE is more than a simple word
    or phrase saying "I DO"

It doesn't really matter if you're small in stature
*   or considered SUPER SIZE*
If you keep the faith in God,
*   you'll receive the ULTIMATE PRIZE*
God's snatched me from the grasps of the devil
*   and opened up my eyes*
He's touched his gentle hands on me
*   and brought me back ALIVE*
And if my eyes never open again
*   to see another sun arise*
I'll cherish rappin' with Baby Ray
*   about the years gone by*
I'll savor all memories good and bad,
*   and I can hold my head up high*
Because I know deep down in my heart
*   that I gave it my best try*
This is THE LAST POEM OR RAP
*   that God's asked me to pass on to you*
With all that said and done…
*   I just want to say, THANK YOU*
I'm overwhelmed with joy
*   that you read about me and my best friend*
But I hope I made a NEW FRIEND
*   who is about to read THE END*

03/24/04